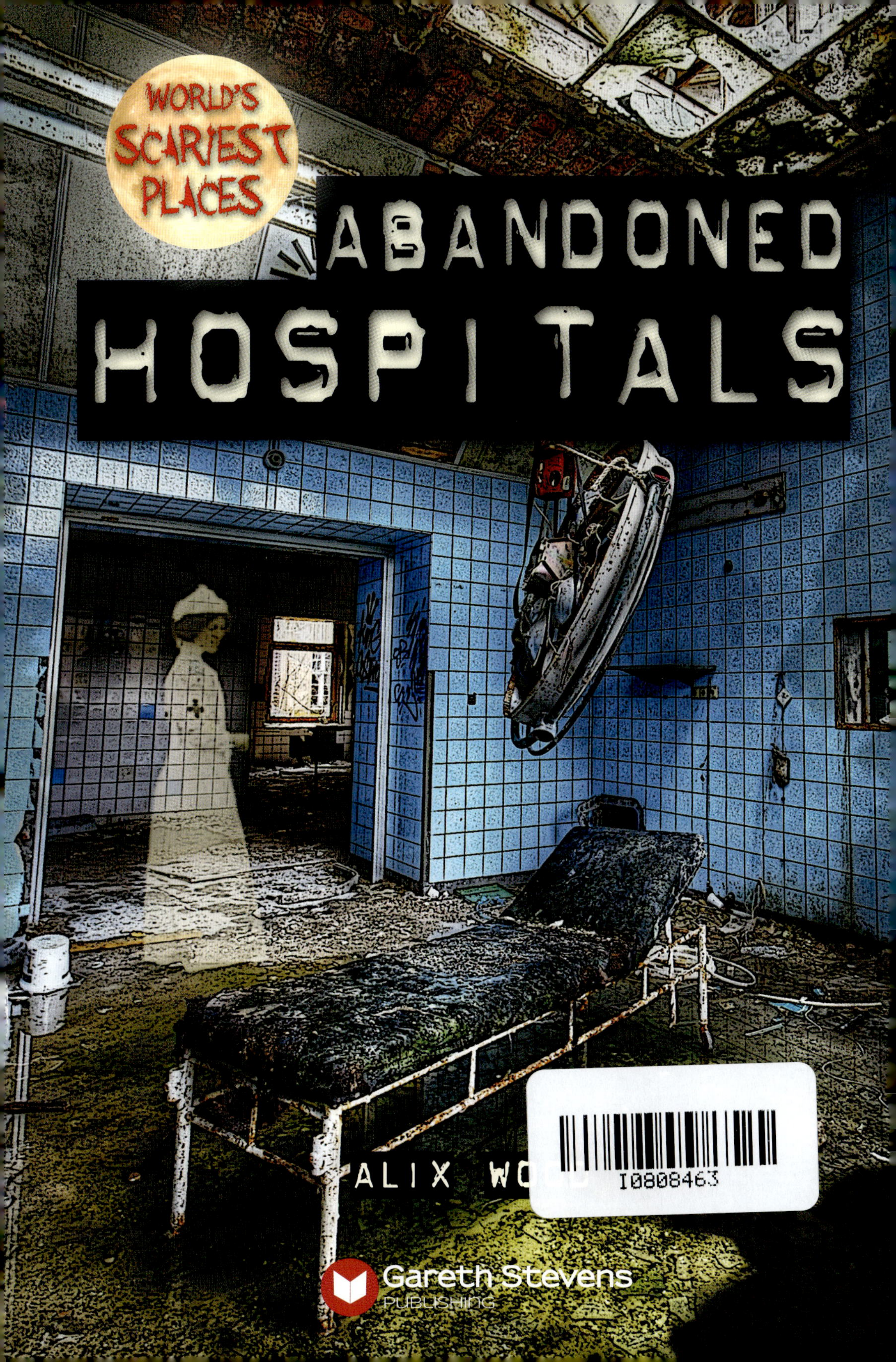

WORLD'S SCARIEST PLACES

ABANDONED HOSPITALS

ALIX WOOD

Gareth Stevens PUBLISHING

Please visit our website, **www.garethstevens.com**. For a free color catalog of all our high-quality books, call toll free 1-800-542-2595 or fax 1-877-542-2596

Cataloging-in-Publication Data

Names: Wood, Alix.

Title: Abandoned hospitals / Alix Wood.

Description: New York : Gareth Stevens, 2017. | Series: World's scariest places | Includes index.

Identifiers: ISBN 9781482458978 (pbk.) | ISBN 9781482458992 (library bound) | ISBN 9781482458985 (6 pack)

Subjects: LCSH: Haunted hospitals--Juvenile literature.

Classification: LCC BF1474.4 W66 2017 | DDC 133.1'22--dc23

First Edition

Published in 2017 by
Gareth Stevens Publishing
111 East 14th Street, Suite 349
New York, NY 10003

Produced for Gareth Stevens by Alix Wood Books
Designed by Alix Wood
Editor: Eloise Macgregor

Cover, 1, 4, 5 bottom, 7 top, 22 © AdobeStock; 3 © Dreamstime; 5 top © Rob Walker; 6 © Jack E. Boucher; 7 bottom, 9 top, 11 top, 15 top, 20 left, 27, 29 top © public domain; 8, 17 right © Shutterstock; 9 bottom © M. Allix; 10-11 © Camilla Canessa; 12 © Brian Jeffery Beggerly; 13 top © Nir Sinay; 13 bottom © 123RF; 14-15 © Eldraque77; 16, 17 left © Dan Lundberg; 18 © Jane Brown; 19 © Frieda Heinrich; 20-21 © British Library; 21 top © Christopher Porter; 23 bottom © National Archives; 23 bottom © Library of Congress; 24-25 © Repton1; 24 bottom © Henry Pascoe; 26 © National Library of Australia; 27 top © State Library of Victoria; 28 © Leslie K. Dellovade; 29 bottom © Hank Stevenson

Printed in China

CPSIA compliance information: Batch #CW17GS. For further information contact Gareth Stevens, New York, New York at 1-800-542-2595.

Contents

Introduction 4
Taunton State Hospital, Massachusetts .. 6
Somerset Hospital, South Africa 8
Poveglia Island, Italy 10
Old Changi Hospital, Singapore.............12
Aradale Mental Hospital, Australia 14
Royal Hope Hospital, Florida 16
BMH Hostert, Germany.......................... 18
Tranquille Sanatorium, Canada 20
Clark Air Base Hospital,
The Philippines 22
Newsham Park Hospital, England 24
Beechworth Asylum, Australia............26
Athens Mental Hospital, Ohio 28
Glossary 30
Further Information 31
Index..32

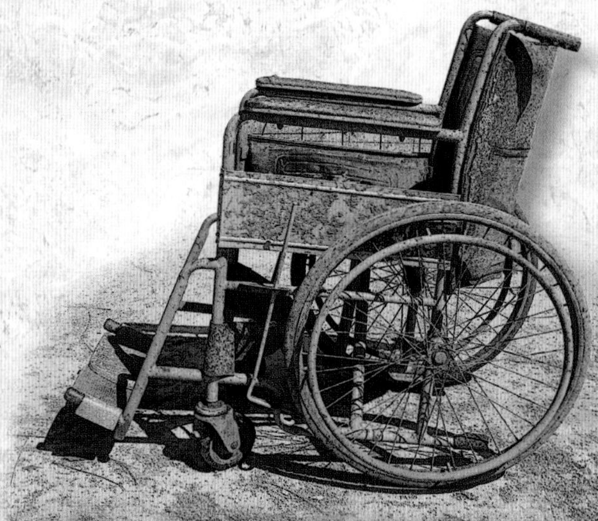

Not everyone believes in ghosts. A ghost is said to be the spirit of someone who has died. Hospitals unfortunately see a lot of death. Ghosts are believed most likely to appear if a person died in unhappy circumstances. Hospitals that treated patients with **mental illness** are often thought to be haunted. The vast, old buildings, and the treatments the patients suffered, were all pretty scary!

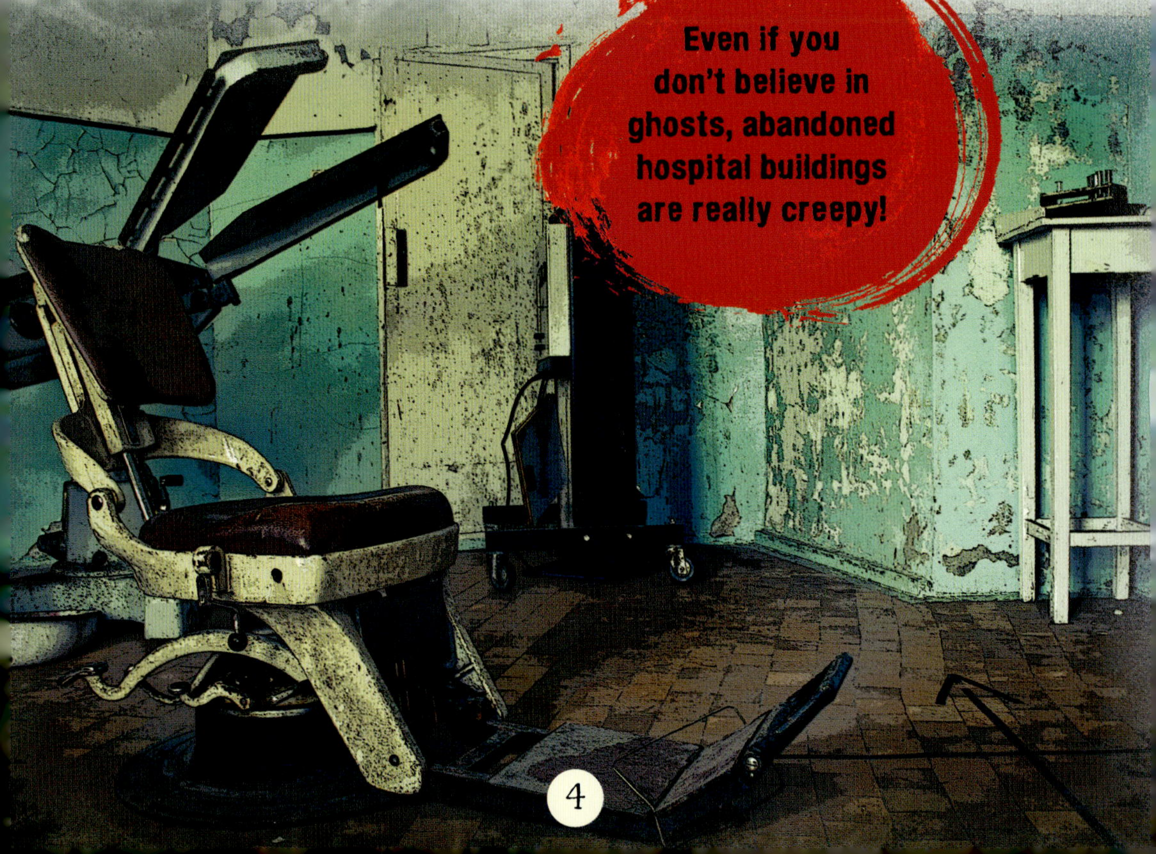

Even if you don't believe in ghosts, abandoned hospital buildings are really creepy!

A LONG, SPOOKY CORRIDOR AT THE ABANDONED SEVERALLS HOSPITAL

Severalls Hospital, England, is an old psychiatric hospital abandoned in 1997. Doctors tested some unusual "cures" on patients here. Ghosts are said to haunt the gardens and the mortuary.

Medical care was often not that good. Hospitals nowadays are much nicer places to be! People didn't know how to treat problems such as mental illness. Treatment was sometimes quite cruel. Perhaps it's not surprising some of the old patients aren't too happy!

Taunton State Hospital, Massachusetts

Taunton State Hospital was built in 1854 as a hospital for the mentally ill. There are rumors that hospital staff would take patients to the basement and make them take part in strange devil-worshipping **rituals**! People have said that they feel very uneasy near the door to the basement.

The nearby woods are also said to be haunted by unexplained banging sounds, moans, strange lights, and icy drafts!

THE OLD HOSPITAL BUILDING

People believe the ghost of a man is often seen on the third floor of the hospital. He is sometimes seen angrily walking along the corridors. Even scarier, his shadow is sometimes seen crawling along the walls!

One of the most violent patients that lived, and died, at Taunton State Hospital was Jane Toppan. Toppan was a nurse who confessed to murdering 31 patients in her care. She was sent to Taunton Insane Hospital, as the hospital was known then. She stayed there for the rest of her life.

Some believe her evil spirit may be responsible for the ghostly events there since her death.

Somerset Hospital, South Africa

South Africa's oldest hospital was built in 1818. The hospital has seen its fair share of births and deaths over the years, and it is believed to be haunted. Night staff in one of the wards believe a ghost must be sitting in one of their chairs. They see the cushion dent, but no one is there!

Sometimes the elevator moves without anyone pressing the button. People have also heard ghostly footsteps behind them, or heard music.

The ghost of a young blonde-haired girl is said to have been seen. She often stands at a window at the top of one of the towers, combing her hair.

The spooky "Lady in Gray" is believed to be the ghost of Sister Henrietta Stockdale (right). Stockdale would sleep in a small room at the top of the building when she visited to train the nurses. Legend has it her ghost has been seen in that room, on the stairs and doing the rounds of the wards.

THE HAUNTED TOWERS OF THE OLD BUILDING

Poveglia Island, Italy

Poveglia is a small island in a **lagoon** near Venice, Italy. In the 1500s, anyone ill with the **plague** was sent to the island to try to keep the disease from spreading. Many thousands of people are believed to have died of plague on the island. Their bodies were burned. Poveglia is thought to be haunted by their ghosts.

The whole island is now empty. Most local people do not like to set foot on the spooky island. Fishermen are known not to like to fish in the area, either, in case they drag up a body!

VENICE LAGOON AND THE ISLAND OF POVEGLIA

In 1922, a mental hospital was established on the island. Local legend says that a doctor at the hospital threw himself from this tower, claiming he had been driven mad by the ghosts.

The ghosts of the many dead former patients are believed to haunt the island. People who have visited the island say that they feel a feeling of evil as soon as they step onto the shore. Visitors have reported hearing screams, and seeing strange shadows.

Old Changi Hospital, Singapore

Originally built by the British military, Old Changi Hospital now lies abandoned. This crumbling building is haunted by a troubled past. The hospital was taken over by the Japanese during World War II and used as a prison. Some prisoners were believed to have been **tortured** in a room at the hospital. When the war was ending, many Japanese soldiers were also **executed** on the grounds.

A small room at Changi has chains fastened to the walls and two concrete blocks on the floor. It is believed to have been the torture room. No one is sure what the concrete blocks were for, but it probably wasn't nice.

ONE OF THE SPOOKY HOSPITAL CORRIDORS

Old Changi Hospital is now believed to be haunted by several ghosts. Screams are sometimes heard along its decaying corridors! Many people have smelled phantom odors, too. Visitors have smelled the scent of almonds, or a musty smell.

A ghostly small boy has been seen sitting, staring into space. People who have seen the boy say they get a strong sense of sadness after seeing him.

Japanese soldiers, covered in blood, are believed to have been seen wandering around the hospital rooms and along the corridors.

Aradale Mental Hospital, Australia

Aradale housed many of the country's most violent and dangerous people. The treatment the patients received was said to have been violent, too. Over the 130 years the hospital was open, 13,000 patients are believed to have died there!

One patient, known as Old Margaret, escaped the hospital when it closed down in the 1990s. Having lived there most of her life, Old Margaret is said to have returned to Aradale to haunt the building. Another ghost haunts the men's wing, and is heard banging on the walls of one of the **isolation** rooms!

THE ENTRANCE TO ARADALE

Walls around the patients' courtyard had what is known as a "ha-ha." A trench ran along the inside of the courtyard. From the outside of the asylum the walls looked low. From inside, the walls were tall and impossible to escape over.

Nurse Kerry is believed to haunt one wing of the hospital. She is said to follow the visitors on ghost tours that now take place around the site!

Royal Hope Hospital, Florida

This Spanish military hospital in St. Augustine, Florida, was unknowingly built on top of an old Native American burial mound. The original building was demolished, but an identical hospital was built back on the same site. The building is said to be haunted, perhaps by hospital patients, or perhaps by angry Native American spirits.

The burial ground was found by workers repairing the water lines. They found thousands of human bones! Many believe that disturbing a burial ground will lead to unhappy spirits appearing.

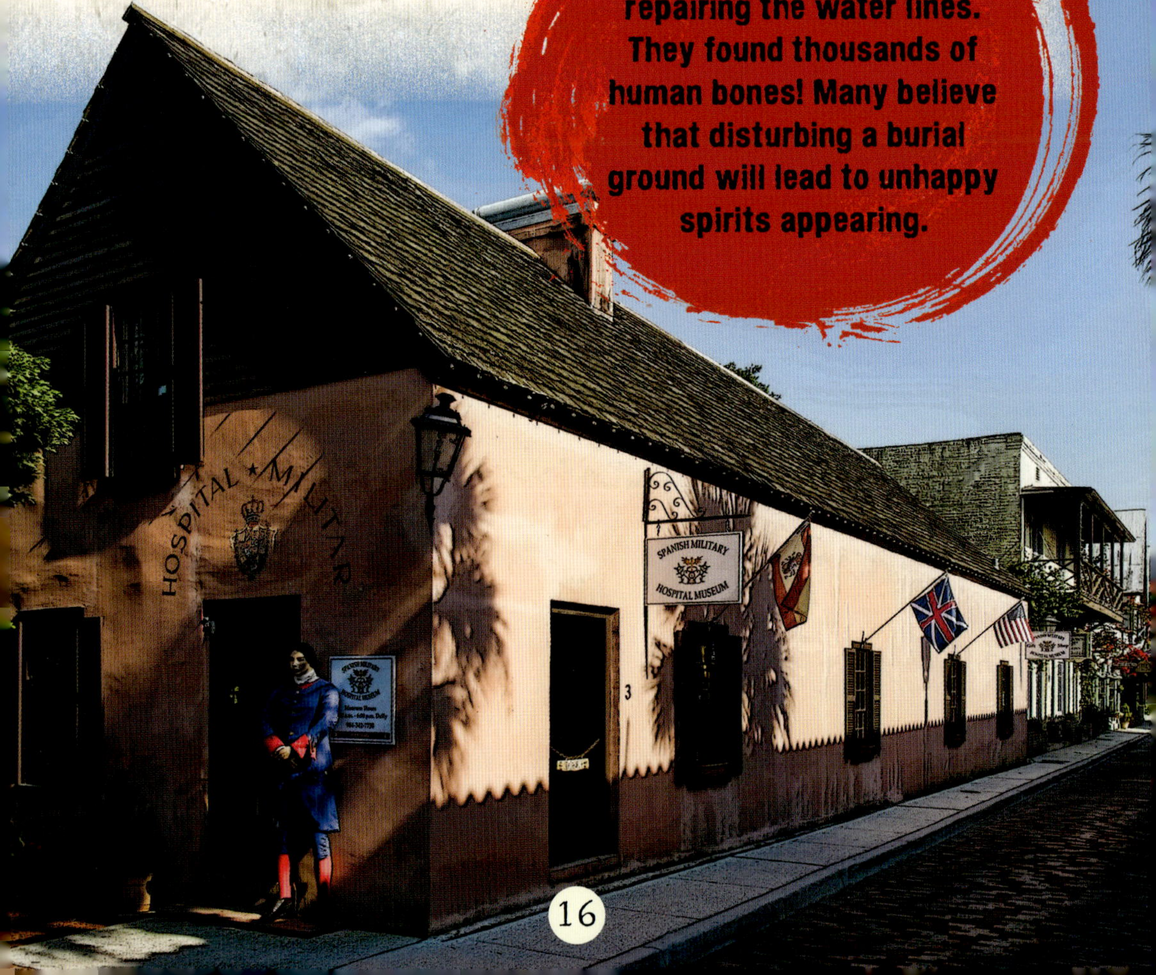

Local rumor is that certain rooms at the old hospital are especially haunted. The Mourning Room was where dying patients were taken in their final hours. Mumbled conversations, cries, and screams can sometimes be heard in this room. People have also said that it appeared as if a person was lying on the bed. The covers appeared indented, as if the impression of a body was lying there!

The surgeon's office, pictured below, is said to be haunted by strange sounds. Objects are sometimes seen to move or shake all by themselves. One visitor experienced feeling as if a hand was gripping her clothes.

BMH Hostert, Germany

Now abandoned, BMH Hostert was a British military hospital in Germany. The building started life as a Franciscan monastery. Before World War II broke out, the monks were taking care of around 600 disabled patients. In 1939, the **Nazis** ordered that any child born with a disability must be reported to them. The Nazis began a program of **euthanasia**, killing any mentally and physically disabled citizens. The monastery at Hostert became a center for such killings.

THE ABANDONED HOSPITAL

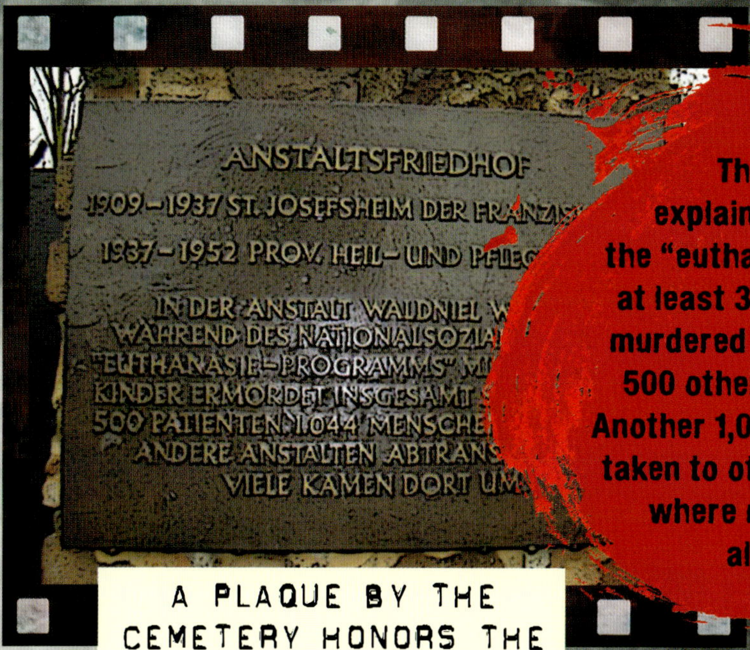

A PLAQUE BY THE CEMETERY HONORS THE MURDERED CHILDREN

This plaque explains that during the "euthanasia-program" at least 30 children were murdered here. More than 500 other patients died. Another 1,044 patients were taken to other institutions, where many of them also died.

After the war, the monastery was leased to the British and turned into a military hospital. In later years the hospital became a British Forces school, although it was kept ready to turn back into a hospital on short notice. This made the building extra spooky for students, as lessons might take place in a tiled morgue, or in the deep cellars where the murders were rumored to have taken place.

The building is said to be haunted by the murdered children. At night screams have been heard, and lights mysteriously glow from rooms with no electricity. In 2014, more children's bones were discovered in the backyard of a local house next to the cemetery.

Tranquille Sanatorium, Canada

Initially built as a ranch, the farmers began to care for people suffering from the disease tuberculosis. Tranquille became a hospital in 1907 and is believed to have cared for over 4,000 patients. Many died of the disease. The hospital closed in the 1950s, but reopened in 1959 to treat mentally ill patients.

There have been many reports of hauntings at the old sanatorium. People have seen flying orbs of light in the buildings. Visitors have experienced a sudden chill in the air, and a very heavy feeling of sadness at the site.

A nurse is said to haunt the site. She is believed to have been murdered by one of the patients.

The sanatorium finally closed in 1983. Since then it has fallen into disrepair. The farm has been bought and the owners run tours of the vast, spooky tunnels that run under the old hospital building.

Another ghost people say haunts the hospital is a mother weeping for her child. If approached, her ghost disappears, but the crying can still be heard! The sound of children crying has also been heard in the children's area of the hospital.

THE TRANQUILLE SITE WAS HUGE AND INCLUDED A FIRE STATION AND STORES!

Clark Air Base Hospital, The Philippines

Clark Air Base was a US military base from 1903 to 1991. The now abandoned hospital building is considered to be the most haunted place in the Philippines. Screams and voices have been heard from the ruins. Strange balls of light have also been seen moving around the building. Battle-scarred ghosts have been seen floating around the building, too!

THE ABANDONED HOSPITAL AT CLARK AIR BASE

Most of the patients treated at Clark Air Base were injured servicemen. Soldiers from both World War II and the Vietnam War were treated there. Many were badly injured, and many died.

The old hospital is guarded by security patrols. One guard doing his rounds on his first night of duty said he heard the sound of heavy boots on the concrete corridor. No one was there. Suddenly a big man in **camouflage** approached him. The man had no face! The ghost asked for a cigarette. When he took it, his hands were ice cold. He then vanished into thin air!

Newsham Park Hospital, England

The boarded-up hospital at Newsham Park, Liverpool, is a very spooky building. Hospital beds, wheelchairs, and gurneys lie rusting and covered in dust. It is a very popular site for ghost tours.

People have experienced cold spots, objects moving and appearing somewhere else, and have heard ghostly whispered voices. Dragging sounds have been heard coming from an empty dining room. Shadowy people have been seen in one ward, and a child has been seen on the top floor.

The building was originally an orphanage for seamen's children. Life at the orphanage was harsh. Along one attic corridor is a row of fourteen "naughty cupboards." Children were locked in the dark cupboards if they had been bad. The cupboards have been known to open and shut by themselves.

A CARVED SHIP ON A BALCONY

One party on a ghost tour parked all their cars on the hospital grounds. When they went back to the cars, some of them had their doors and windows open. All the cars had been securely locked with the windows and doors shut! Also, oddly, none of the cars' alarms had gone off.

Many people died in the building over the years. Mysteriously, a 19-year-old servant named Florence Hansford was found dead in one of the park's lakes on New Year's Day, 1897. Perhaps her ghost haunts the hospital today?

Beechworth Asylum, Australia

Beechworth was home to around 1,200 patients at its peak. It was easy to get admitted to the asylum. It was not so easy to leave. Some spooky things have happened at the asylum. Jars of patient's body parts were kept in the laboratory. In the 1950s, during some construction work, the jars all disappeared. Some believe the gruesome jars may now be stored in a walled-up part of the cellars.

BEECHWORTH ASYLUM AROUND 1950

A woman drowned in this fountain in front of the asylum. The fountain is no longer there, but can be seen in this photo from 1906. Another woman was pushed to her death from the third floor window, apparently after a fight over a pack of cigarettes!

Matron Sharpe is said to still wander on the grounds of the old asylum. Her ghost has been seen in several parts of the hospital. The old building is now used as part of Latrobe University. Matron Sharpe has been seen in the dormitory area, and students have seen her in the computer rooms! She has also been spotted on the granite staircase and in one of the classrooms.

Matron Sharpe was quite a caring nurse to the patients. She is remembered for brightening the asylum up with lace doilies, pretty drapes, and vases of fresh flowers.

Athens Mental Hospital, Ohio

More than 1,900 people are buried in the cemetery at Athens Mental Hospital. Most of their graves are just marked by a number! The hospital became known for being a center for a practice known as lobotomy. This was a type of brain surgery that used to be done, intending to calm mental patients. Many died during the operation.

Many of the old hospital buildings are now used by Ohio University. Students sometimes see ghostly figures and hear screams!

THE MAIN HOSPITAL BUILDING IS NOW A CAMPUS ART MUSEUM.

STAFF PHOTOGRAPHED ON THE HOSPITAL'S OPENING DAY

When Athens Mental Hospital first opened in 1874, staff cared mostly for Civil War soldiers suffering from what we know now as **post-traumatic stress disorder**. The care given by the staff was very good.

THE STAINED FLOOR

The care went downhill a little over the years. In 1979, patient Margaret Schilling went missing. Her body was found 42 days later locked in an old unused ward! Over time her body had stained the concrete floor and the mark remains to this day. Her ghost is still said to haunt Ward 20 today.

Glossary

camouflage A patterned material that helps people hide.

euthanasia Killing sick or injured people.

executed Put to death as a punishment.

isolation Kept separate from others.

lagoon A stretch of salt water separated from the sea by a sandbank or reef.

mental illness A serious disorder in a person's behavior or thinking.

mortuary A place in which the bodies of the dead are kept until their burial.

Nazis Members of a German fascist party controlling Germany from 1933 to 1945.

orphanage A place caring for children whose parents have died.

plague A serious disease causing a high rate of death.

post-traumatic stress disorder Anxiety caused by frightening or distressing events.

psychiatric A branch of medicine that deals with disorders of the mind, emotions, or behavior.

rituals Ceremonial acts.

tortured Punished or forced to do or say something by causing great pain.

Further Information

Williams, Dinah. *Monstrous Morgues of the Past (Scary Places)*. New York, NY: Bearport Publishing, 2011.

Williams, Dinah. *Shuttered Horror Hospitals (Scary Places)*. New York, NY: Bearport Publishing, 2014.

Website

Ducksters site with information about hospitals during the American Civil War:

www.ducksters.com/history/civil_war/medicine.php

Publisher's note to educators and parents:
Our editors have carefully reviewed these websites to ensure that they are suitable for students. Many websites change frequently, however, and we cannot guarantee that a site's future contents will continue to meet our high standards of quality and educational value. Be advised that students should be closely supervised whenever they access the Internet.

Index

Aradale Mental Hospital 14, 15
Athens Mental Hospital 28, 29

Beechworth Asylum 26, 27
BMH Hostert 18, 19

Clark Air Base Hospital 22, 23
crawling man, the 7

Hansford, Florence 25

Newsham Park Hospital 24, 25
Nurse Kerry 15

Old Changi Hospital 12, 13
Old Margaret 14

Poveglia Island 10, 11

Royal Hope Hospital 16, 17
Schilling, Margaret 29
Severalls Hospital 5
Sharpe, Matron 27
Somerset Hospital 8, 9
St. Augustine burial mound 16
Stockdale, Sister Henrietta 9

Taunton State Hospital 6, 7
Toppan, Jane 7
Tranquille Sanatorium 20, 21

Don't be scared! Most people don't believe ghosts are real at all. No one has ever scientifically proven they exist. But it can be fun to get yourself a little spooked!